Using Literature To Learn About Children Around The World

A Thematic Approach To Cultural Awareness

by Judith Cochran

Incentive Publications, Inc.
Nashville, Tennessee

Illustrated by Marta Johnson
Cover by Susan Eaddy
Edited by Rebecca Newton

ISBN 0-86530-261-8

Table of Contents

Week One

Week Two

Student Activity Pages

PREFACE

This ready-to-use thematic unit provides everything an educator needs to teach a fully-integrated two-week-long course of study of children around the world, including lesson plans, teacher's guide, and student reproducible worksheets. Many school systems now base their curricula on broad themes and student outcomes, a practice which allows teachers a great deal of flexibility when selecting units. Instead of textbooks, today's teaching books of choice are often literature books and information books. The topics are broad so that children will learn all of the basics — in this book there are specific activities in every subject, including Reading, Writing, Math, Science, Social Studies, and Art. All of the work of pulling together information and legend theory into an integrated whole has been done for you.

This study of children around the world need not be presented in strict accordance with the outlined two-week schedule. There are many ways to use this book! The unit is so packed with activities and information, it can easily extend to longer than two weeks. Some educators prefer to spend at least two days on a literature book, even if it is a short primary-level book. You may include information books with your literature lessons so that children may do research, writing, and presentations along with their activities. *Using Literature To Learn About Children Around The World* is also an invaluable resource for a traditional textbook-driven classroom, as it enriches, reinforces skills, educates, and provides across-the-curriculum activities and opportunities for further study and growth.

Each lesson is detailed in the teacher's guide pages (11–52) with concepts broken down into an easy-to-follow format. Student activity pages (53–76) are easy to understand and ready to use as reproducible blackline masters. For further study, additional books and projects are suggested (77– 79).

The people and the customs of six continents are presented:
- North America
- South America
- Europe
- Asia
- Africa
- Australia

(Even though there are seven continents, Antarctica has no indigenous people.)

The books you will need for this unit are:

    <u>All In A Day</u>, by Mitsumasa Anno, et al. Philomel Books, NY, 1986.

    <u>Anno's Britain</u>, by Mitsumasa Anno. Philomel Books, NY, 1982.

    <u>Rechenka's Eggs</u>, by Patricia Polacco. Philomel Books, NY, 1988.

    <u>The Empty Pot</u>, by Demi. Holt, NY, 1990.

    <u>Crow Boy</u>, by Taro Yashima. Puffin Books, NY, 1955.

    <u>My Grandma Lived In Gooligulch</u>, by Graeme Base. Australian Book Source, Davis, California, 1988.

    <u>On The Pampas</u>, by Maria Cristina Brusca. Holt, New York, 1991.

    <u>Mufaro's Beautiful Daughters</u>, by John Steptoe. William Morrow and Co., New York, 1987.

    <u>Once A Mouse</u>, by Marcia Brown. Aladdin Books, New York, 1961.

    <u>Where The Children Live</u>, by Thomas B. Allen. Prentice-Hall, New Jersey, 1980.

Special materials required for various activities are:

- British tea ingredients (page 16)
- Eggs for Science experiment (page 20)
- Borscht and Pashka ingredients (page 22)
- Snow pea pods and rulers for math (page 24)
- Seeds for planting and observation (page 25)
- Chinese New Year Dragon material (page 26)
- Chopsticks, vegetables, rice and cooking utensils (page 30)
- Fish print materials (page 31)
- Shadow puppet theatre (page 48)
- Curry ingredients (page 50)
- Globes, world wall map, magazines, white shelf paper, plastic straws, toilet paper tubes, wire hangers, watercolor brushes, tissue and wrapping paper, tagboard, beans, and shoeboxes for various projects.

Sending this list home to parents as a "wish list" can be helpful.

READY-TO-USE THEMATIC UNIT OUTLINE (WEEK ONE)

MONDAY	TUESDAY	WEDNESDAY	THURSDAY	FRIDAY
The World (Seven Continents)	Europe (Britain)	Asia (Ukraine & Russia)	Asia (China)	Asia (Japan)
READ ALOUD: All in a Day (Anno, et al) Teacher Page 11	**READ ALOUD:** Anno's Britain (Anno) Teacher Page 15	**READ ALOUD:** Rechenka's Eggs (Polacco) Teacher Page 19	**READ ALOUD:** The Empty Pot (Demi) Teacher Page 23	**READ ALOUD:** Crow Boy (Yashima) Teacher Page 29
WRITING: Questioning: Write questions students want to ask children of other countries Teacher Page 11	**WRITING:** Expository Writing: What do you know about Britain? Teacher Page 15	**WRITING:** Dialogue Between Babushka & Goose Teacher Page 19 Student Page 60	**WRITING:** Predicting Outcomes: Was Ping a good emperor? Teacher Page 23	**WRITING:** Haiku Poems Teacher Page 29
READING EXPERIENCE: Comprehension, Similarities/Differences Teacher Page 11	**READING EXPERIENCE:** British & American Words Teacher Page 15 Student Page 56	**READING EXPERIENCE:** Summarizing/Finger Puppets Teacher Page 20 Student Page 61	**READING EXPERIENCE:** Story Map: Characters, Problem, Solution Teacher Page 23	**ACTIVITY CHOICES:** Cooking & Eating w/Chopsticks Teacher Page 30
MATH: Telling Time Teacher Page 12 Student Page 53	**MATH:** Compute-and-Color British Flag Teacher Page 16 Student Page 57	**MATH:** Patterning Puzzles Teacher Page 20 Student Page 62	**MATH:** Estimation/Measuring/Graphing Snow Pea Pods Teacher Page 24	Origami Teacher Page 30 Student Page 65
SOCIAL STUDIES: Continents Teacher Page 13 Student Page 54	**SCIENCE:** Tea Teacher Page 16	**SCIENCE:** Parts of an Egg Teacher Page 20 Student Page 63	**SCIENCE:** Seeds & the Chinese Teacher Page 25 Student Page 64	European & Asian Games Teacher Page 30
ART: Flags of North America Teacher Page 14 Student Page 55	**SOCIAL STUDIES:** Map, Britain's History Teacher Page 17 Student Page 58	**SOCIAL STUDIES:** Map, Life in Russia/Ukraine, Borscht & Pashka Teacher Page 21 Student Page 58	**SOCIAL STUDIES:** Map, Chinese New Year Teacher Page 26 Student Page 58	**SCIENCE:** Fish Prints Teacher Page 31
	ART: Tower of London Teacher Page 18 Student Page 59	**ART:** Egg Mobile Teacher Page 22	**ART:** Chinese Characters Teacher Page 28	**SOCIAL STUDIES:** Map, Japanese Songs & Customs Teacher Page 32 Student Page 58

READY-TO-USE THEMATIC UNIT OUTLINE (WEEK TWO)

MONDAY	TUESDAY	WEDNESDAY	THURSDAY	FRIDAY
Australia	South America	Africa	Asia (India)	Houses Around The World
READ ALOUD: My Grandma Lived In Gooligulch (Base) Teacher Page 33	**READ ALOUD:** On The Pampas (Brusca) Teacher Page 37	**READ ALOUD:** Mufaro's Beautiful Daughters (Steptoe) Teacher Page 41	**READ ALOUD:** Once A Mouse (Brown) Teacher Page 45	**READ ALOUD:** Where The Children Live (Allen) Teacher Page 49
WRITING: Poem: Tell About Own Grandma Teacher Page 33	**WRITING:** Similarities/Differences Between Cowboys & Gauchos Teacher Page 37	**WRITING:** Research & Expository Writing About Zimbabwe Teacher Page 41	**WRITING:** Chart Story: Tigers Teacher Page 45	**WRITING:** Semantic Mapping: Where do you live? Teacher Page 49
READING EXPERIENCE: Drawing Conclusions: What happened to Grandma? Teacher Page 33	**READING EXPERIENCE:** Fold Book: Vacation Album Teacher Page 37 Student Page 69	**READING EXPERIENCE:** Research Teacher Page 41	**READING EXPERIENCE:** Sequencing Story Events Teacher Page 45 Student Page 73	**ACTIVITY CHOICES:** Dioramas Tchr Page 50 Flags Tchr Page 50 Student Page 76 Curry Tchr Page 50 Act Out Stories, Songs, Poems & Dances Tchr Page 51
MATH: Great Barrier Reef Calculations Teacher Page 34 Student Page 66	**MATH:** Map Reading Teacher Page 38 Student Page 70	**MATH:** Hieroglyphic Code Teacher Page 41 Student Page 72	**MATH:** Discrimination: The Taj Mahal Teacher Page 46 Student Page 74	**Culminating Activities:**
SCIENCE: Triarama: Australia's Animals Teacher Page 34 Student Page 67	**SCIENCE:** The Rain Forests Teacher Page 38	**SCIENCE:** African Animal Mix-up Teacher Page 42	**SCIENCE:** The Himalayas Teacher Page 46	**SCIENCE:** Poster, Enjoy Curry Teacher Page 51
SOCIAL STUDIES: Map, Aborigines, Dream Dancing Teacher Page 35 Student Page 58	**SOCIAL STUDIES:** Map, Save the Rain Forests Poster Teacher Page 39 Student Page 58	**SOCIAL STUDIES:** Map, Egypt/Ghana & Swahili Teacher Page 43 Student Page 58	**SOCIAL STUDIES:** Map, Hindu Festivals Teacher Page 47 Student Page 58	**SOCIAL STUDIES:** Map, Unit Folder Teacher Page 52 Student Page 58
ART: Aboriginal Art Teacher Page 36 Student Page 68	**ART:** Amazon Headdress Teacher Page 39 Student Page 71	**ART:** Drums, Rattles, Chants Teacher Page 44	**ART:** Shadow Puppets Teacher Page 48 Student Page 75	**ART:** Perform Stories, Songs, Poems & Dances Art Show of Unit Projects Teacher Page 52

10

All In A Day

by Anno, et al

READ ALOUD: Whole Group

Before Reading Activity

While you are in school, what do you think other children around the world are doing? (Discuss.)

This book is about what children around the world are doing on New Year's Day. Listen to the story and find out what the children are doing, what their homes are like, and what the weather is like.

Teacher Reads Aloud

All In A Day, by Anno, et al.

After Reading Activity

What were the children doing? What were their homes like and how was the weather? (Discuss.)

WRITING: Whole Group or Small Groups

Group Activity

Questioning: After reading the book, what questions would you want to ask the children from the different countries? (List on board. Model writing sentences from student responses.) Then discuss how students might answer the same questions about their own country.

Pre-Writers: Draw a picture showing a question you would ask a child from another country. Copy a question from the board.

Beginning Writers: Draw and write one or two questions you would ask someone from another country.

Experienced Writers: Write all the questions you would ask a child from another country. Answer them about yourself if you have time. Illustrate your work.

READING EXPERIENCE: Whole Group, Small or Cooperative Groups, Pairs

You Will Need:
- book: All In A Day, by Anno, et al
- 8½" x 11" blank paper (one per child)
- pencils
- crayons

Comprehension

Before Reading Activity: On the board, list the eight countries the book is about (i.e., USA, England, Russia, Japan, Brazil, Kenya, China, Australia). Discuss what was happening in each of these places on New Year's Day.

Listen and look at the book again to see what is happening in each country.

Teacher Reads Aloud: All In A Day, by Anno, et al.

After Reading Activity: What was happening in each country? (Draw and list the activities under each heading on the board. Discuss similarities and differences.)

Similarities/Differences

Student Assignment:
Fold paper into fourths. Draw (and write if possible) what children in four countries were doing on New Year's Day. Then with a partner, discuss the similarities and differences between countries including our own.

MATH: Whole Group, Small or Cooperative Groups

You Will Need:
- Student Page 53
- pencils
- scissors
- paste

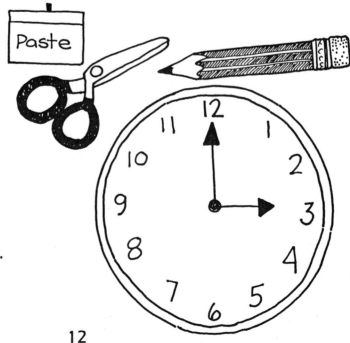

Telling Time

1. Teach students to tell time to the hour (big hand on the 12, little hand on the hour).

2. Teach them how to properly write the time. (1:00 = one o'clock.)

3. Once they have mastered those concepts, have them problem-solve what time it would be in an hour, two hours, etc. Teach them how to use the clock face to count the number of hours ahead.

Student Page 53: Work along with students to help them problem-solve each section of the page. The point of this exercise is not how many right or wrong answers they get, but understanding the process used to arrive at the answer.

SOCIAL STUDIES: Whole Group

- You Will Need:
- Student Page 54
- crayons

The Continents

1. There are seven continents on the earth:

   North America
   South America
   Europe
   Africa
   Asia
   Australia
   Antarctica

   Note: To help students recall the continents' names, simply remember six A's plus one E.

2. People inhabit only six of the seven continents because Antarctica is too cold.

Student Page 54: Have children read the map. Discuss which continents are in which hemispheres. Australia and Antarctica are the only ones completely in the southern hemisphere. Have children follow directions for coloring the continents.

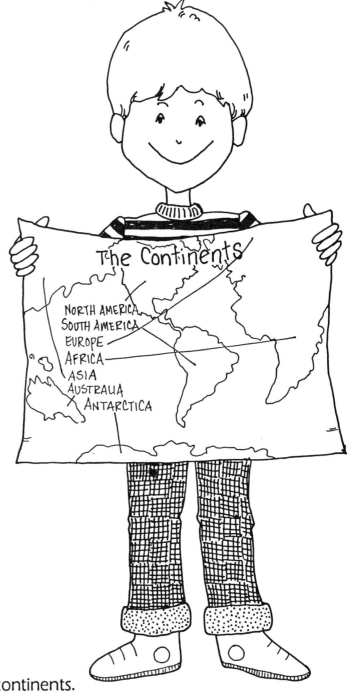

ART: Whole Group

You Will Need:
- Student Page 55
- plastic drinking straws (three per child)
- scissors
- crayons
- paste

Flags of North America

1. The three largest countries in North America are: Canada, the United States, and Mexico. Each country has its own flag.

2. Canada's flag is red and white. It has a red maple leaf in the center which is the symbol of Canada.

3. The United States flag is red, white, and blue. There are thirteen stripes that stand for the original thirteen colonies, and fifty stars standing for each state in the country.

4. Mexico's flag is green, white, and red. In the center is a picture of an eagle with its claws on a snake. According to a legend, the Aztec Indians of Mexico built their most important city where an eagle held a snake in its claws.

Student Page 55: The children color and cut out the flags. Then they fold and paste each one around a plastic drinking straw.

Note: To stand the flags up, set them in a small ball of modeling clay.

Anno's Britain

by Mitsumasa Anno

READ ALOUD: Whole Group

Before Reading Activity

Just as some people live in small towns and some in big cities in Canada or in the United States, people live the same way in Britain.

This book has only pictures. Look carefully at the types of buildings people live in and the things they do.

Teacher Reads Aloud

Anno's Britain, by Mitsumasa Anno.

After Reading Activity

What types of buildings did you see? What kinds of things did the people do? (Discuss and write on board.)

WRITING: Whole Group or Small Groups

Group Activity

Expository Writing: What do you know about Britain? (Look at list generated in the After Reading Activity.) Then thumb through Anno's Britain again and have children look closer at buildings, animals, and what people are doing. (Make sure to draw attention to Stonehenge's standing stones and Britain's castles.) Generate discussion and list more things on the board. (Model writing sentences from phrases on board about Britain.)

Pre-Writers: Draw a picture about something people in Britain do. Copy a sentence from the board, or copy and complete the sentence:
"In Britain they _____."

Beginning Writers: Draw and write one or two things about Britain.

Experienced Writers: Write a paragraph about Britain. Illustrate your work when done.

READING EXPERIENCE: Whole Group, Small, or Cooperative Groups

You Will Need:
- Student Page 56   • crayons
- pencils

Comprehension
British and American Words

The "Queen's English" and American English have interesting differences.

Student Page 56: With the teacher's help, students read through the British words and their American equivalents. They write the British words for pictures at the bottom of the page. Then in pairs or small groups, children use the British words in conversation and have others translate the meaning in American terms.

MATH: Whole Group or Small Groups

You Will Need:
- Student Page 57
- pencils
- crayons

Compute-and-Color British Flag

The British flag is known as the "Union Jack." It is a compilation of three flags—England's cross of St. George, Scotland's St. Andrew's cross, and Ireland's cross of St. Patrick.

Student Page 57: Students compute the equations given in each section of the flag. If the answer is 5, they color the section red. If it is 7, the section is to be colored blue.

SCIENCE: Whole Group

You Will Need:

- tea bags
- scissors
- cucumbers/tomatoes/lettuce
- spreadable margarine
- white bread
- milk

- plastic spoons
- paring and spreading knives
- paper cups, plates, napkins
- large kettle for tea
- sugar cubes
- serving plates

Tea

1. Tea is the national drink of Britain. It comes from China and is made from the dried leaves of a tea bush. There are many different kinds of tea bushes and many different flavors of tea. Tea is served hot with an option of hot milk and sugar. "Black or white" tea means without milk or with milk.

2. Dissect a tea bag: Cut open a tea bag and give each child a few leaves of tea. Have them smell it, look at it, taste the leaves, and discuss their findings. Record them on the board.

3. Tea time is a snack time in Britain, a tradition begun about one hundred years ago by a princess who got hungry between lunch time and the late dinner time. She began having a small snack with some tea at about five o'clock in the evening, and the practice is still around today.

Formal or "high" tea consists of finger sandwiches (cucumber, tomato, and lettuce), berries and "clotted cream" (like thick whipping cream), biscuits (cookies), and tea.

4. Finger sandwiches (cucumber, tomato and lettuce): Have children peel cucumbers and slice thin, slice tomatoes thin, and peel off leaves of lettuce. Cut off crusts of white bread, spread with thin layer of margarine, then place either a few slices of cucumber, tomato, or leaves of lettuce on it. Top with another buttered slice of crustless bread. Cut diagonally into triangles.

5. Place finger sandwiches and cookies on serving trays. Serve hot tea with choice of milk (called white tea) and sugar cubes ("one lump or two?").

6. Children enjoy their tea while using their best manners and using British words learned during the Reading Experience.

SOCIAL STUDIES: Whole Group

You Will Need:
- Student Page 58
- crayons
- world wall map

Map

1. Britain is made up of four countries: England, Scotland, Wales, and Northern Ireland.

2. Even though Britain is an island nation, it is part of the continent of Europe.

3. The continent of Europe is made up of many countries that speak many different languages. Use the wall map to show the many countries in Europe.

Note: There are many excellent children's books and stories dealing with other European countries. Some are listed at the end of this book. For the purposes of this unit, Britain is the only European country studied.

Student Page 58: Have students find Britain on the map and color it. Color the rest of Europe another color.

Britain's History

1. Britain has an extremely long and colorful history that goes back thousands of years. Long before people knew how to read and write, giant stones were put in circles around Britain. The most famous of these is called Stonehenge. No one knows who put them there or why, but the

circles seem to have astronomic alignments with the sun and moon.

2. The Romans later conquered Britain, but they were unable to subdue the fierce tribes of the north in present day Scotland. They finally built Hadrian's Wall to keep the tribes' marauding bands at bay.

3. Britain was once ruled by kings and queens. Stories of King Arthur and his knights of the round table have become British legend. In one story, Arthur pulled a sword out of a stone to become king. There is some archaeological evidence to support the fact that an ancient king united regional factions. As for the round table, no one knows.

4. Present-day Britain was founded by William the Conqueror in A.D. 1066. The castle he built makes up part of the Tower of London. The "Bloody Tower," as it was later known, was turned into a prison and has housed many famous people. Ruins of many castles, manor houses, and churches are all over Britain. Anno's Britain includes illustrations of the ruins.

5. Britain still has a queen today. Her name is Elizabeth, but she does not run the country anymore. If you were to meet her, the boys would have to bow and the girls would have to curtsy. After Queen Elizabeth dies, her son Charles will become king. When that happens, the people will shout, "The queen is dead. Long live the king!"

6. Britain has produced many great writers like Shakespeare and Charles Dickens. Shakespeare wrote many plays, including Romeo and Juliet. Dickens wrote about Tiny Tim and Scrooge in a book called A Christmas Carol.

ART: Whole Group

You Will Need:
- Student Page 59   ▪ scissors   ▪ crayons   ▪ paste

Tower of London

The Tower of London has a long history. It was built as a castle almost 1,000 years ago. Since then it has been used as a prison where many famous and infamous people were held. King Henry VIII had two of his wives imprisoned there. They were accused of witchcraft and executed by having their heads chopped off with an axe. Today the tower is a museum. It is where the crown jewels (all the jewelry and crowns made for the kings and queens of England) are kept. It is guarded by men called Beefeaters who wear special uniforms.

Student Page 59: The children color the tower, crown jewels, Beefeater and queen, and cut them out. Then they fold each piece at the specified places and paste them together to form a three-dimensional model. They can arrange them and act out stories in small groups.

Rechenka's Eggs

by Patricia Polacco

READ ALOUD: Whole Group

Before Reading Activity
Have you ever seen colorful eggs decorated with many designs? That practice was started in a country called the Ukraine long ago.

This is the story of Babushka and a miracle about the eggs. Listen to the story.

Teacher Reads Aloud
Rechenka's Eggs, by Patricia Polacco.

After Reading Activity
What was the miracle that happened in the story?

WRITING: Whole Group or Small Groups

You Will Need:
- Student Page 60
- pencils
- crayons

Group Activity
Dialogue Between Babushka and the Goose
Discuss what the goose might want to say to Babushka and what Babushka might say to the goose according to the events in the story. (Model writing sentences from children's responses.)

Note: This is a good time to introduce quotation marks to experienced writers.

Student Page 60: Students write what each character would say to the other.

Pre-Writers: Copy a sentence from the board for each character. Draw a picture to go with it.

Beginning Writers: Write what the goose would say to Babushka and what Babushka would say to the goose. Color the pictures when you are finished.

Experienced Writers: Use quotation marks around the words you think both characters would say to the other. Add more illustrations when you are done.

READING EXPERIENCE: Whole Group, Small or Cooperative Groups

Before Reading Activity
Discuss what happened in the story and the sequence in which the events occur. Have children listen to the story again.

Teacher Reads Aloud
Rechenka's Eggs, by Patricia Polacco.

After Reading Activity
Discuss the events in the story.

Summarizing/Finger Puppets
You Will Need:
- Student Page 61
- book: Rechenka's Eggs, by Polacco
- crayons
- scissors
- paste

Student Page 61: Children color, cut out, and paste together the finger puppets. Then tell children to act out the story in small groups using the finger puppets.

MATH: Whole Group or Small Groups

You Will Need:
- Student Page 62
- scissors
- crayons
- paste

Patterning Puzzles
The Ukraine is known for its elaborately colored eggs. The city of Moscow (Moskva in book) in Russia is famous for its "onion domed" buildings. Nesting dolls known as "matryoshka" are also a popular folk art. All of these are used in this exercise.

Student Page 62: Children finish the patterns on the Ukrainian eggs, then cut out and arrange pieces of the mosque puzzle. Then they cut out the nesting dolls and paste them in order, from largest to smallest.

SCIENCE: Whole Group or Small Groups

You Will Need:
- Student Page 63
- crayons
- pencils
- small glass bowls/custard cups
- black construction paper
- chicken eggs

Parts of an Egg
You may examine the parts of a real egg as a whole group or in small groups. Placing glass custard cups on black paper makes all the parts more visible.

Asia: The Ukraine and Russia

1. Carefully break a chicken egg into a small glass bowl sitting on black paper.

2. Point out the different parts of the egg. Note that the chalaza appears as a ribbony white material next to the yolk when out of the shell.

3. Discuss the different animals born from eggs. Note: Ruth Heller's book Chickens Aren't the Only Ones discusses the various animals that hatch from eggs.

Student Page 63: Children first follow the directions and color the parts of an egg. Then they draw what the egg looks like in the glass dish and identify the different parts. The last activity asks them to draw pictures of different animals hatched from eggs.

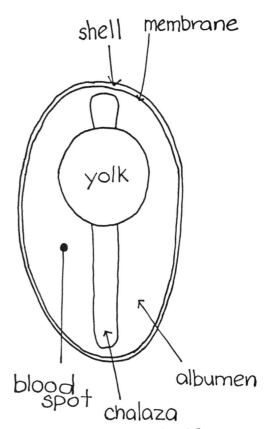

SOCIAL STUDIES: Whole Group

You Will Need:

- Student Page 58
- 4 cans consommé
- 4 cans cream of chicken soup
- 4 cans shoestring beets
- ½ cup raisins
- hot plate
- large cooking pot
- 1 pint sour cream

- paper bowls and plates
- plastic spoons and knives
- 1-2 loaves Russian Rye or Pumpernickel bread
- 8-oz. jar cheese spread
- mixing bowl
- serving and mixing spoons
- blender

Map

Locate the continent of Asia on the map (Student Page 58). Then locate the countries of Russia and the Ukraine. Color them.

Life in Russia and the Ukraine

These countries were once part of the USSR. Now they are independent states in a tentative commonwealth.

1. The children go to school to learn to read and write their own language but they also learn to read and write English. They play games like soccer.

2. In the Ukraine and in Russia, money is called "rubles." These two republics are rich in mineral resources—manufacturing is highly developed and diversified.

3. There are many problems with the new independent countries, but people are working together to solve them.

Borscht and Pashka

Borscht is a beet soup served throughout Russia and the Ukraine. Pashka is a sweet cheese/butter spread used for festive occasions.

Borscht: Combine 4 cans of beets and juice in blender and blend. In a large cooking pot, combine blended beets with 4 cans cream of chicken soup and 4 cans consommé. Heat and serve in paper bowls, topped with a dollop of sour cream.

Pashka: Combine 1-lb. tub spreadable margarine with 8-oz. jar cheese spread and ½ cup raisins in mixing bowl. Spread on Russian Rye or Pumpernickel bread and serve with borscht.

ART: Whole Group

You Will Need:
- egg templates
- wire clothes hangers (one per child)
- white construction paper
- colored felt pens
- tagboard
- dark thread
- scissors

Egg Mobile

Making intricate designs on eggs is a folk art dating back hundreds of years in the Ukraine.

Student Assignment:

1. Make egg templates by cutting several sizes of egg-shaped patterns out of tagboard.

2. Children trace around templates on white construction paper to make five eggs each.

3. Each child decorates both sides of the eggs, then cuts them out and ties them with string of varying lengths to a wire clothes hanger. Make sure each tests the balance of his or her mobile so that it hangs straight.

The Empty Pot

by Demi

READ ALOUD: Whole Group

Before Reading Activity

Would you be honest even if it meant you might get in trouble? (Discuss.)

This is a story about a boy named Ping who lived in China. He has to choose whether or not to be honest. Listen to what happens to him and how he is the same and different from you.

Teacher Reads Aloud

The Empty Pot, by Demi.

After Reading Activity

What did Ping do about being honest? (Discuss.) How is he the same as and different from you? (Discuss.)

WRITING: Whole Group or Small Groups

Group Activity: Predicting Outcomes

Do you think Ping would make a good emperor? Why, why not? (Discuss and list ideas on board. Model writing sentences from student responses.)

Pre-Writers: Draw a picture showing what kind of emperor Ping would be. Copy sentence from the board, or copy and complete this sentence: "Ping would be a _____ emperor because _____."

Beginning Writers: Draw and write about what kind of emperor Ping would be and why.

Experienced Writers: Write a paragraph explaining what kind of emperor Ping would be and why. Illustrate your work when done.

READING EXPERIENCE: Whole Group, Small or Cooperative Groups

You Will Need:
- book: The Empty Pot, by Demi
- writing paper 8½" x 11"
- pencils

Story Map

This activity deals with the characters, problem and solution presented in the story.

Before Reading Activity

Who were the characters in the story? What was the problem Ping had to face in the story? How did he solve it? Listen for these things in the story again.

Teacher Reads Aloud

The Empty Pot, by Demi.

After Reading Activity

Who were the characters in the story? What was the problem Ping had to face? What was the solution? (Discuss and list on board.)

Student Assignment: Children fold paper into horizontal fourths. Tell each child to write his or her name and the title and author of the book on the first quarter. On the second quarter, write the word "Characters," and across from it list and draw the characters in the story. In the third quarter, write the word "Problem." Across from it, write and illustrate the problem in the story. In the last quarter write "Solution," then write and draw the solution of the story.

MATH: Whole Group, Small or Cooperative Groups

You Will Need:
- 8½" x 11" blank paper (one per child)
- snow pea pods (one per child)
- pencils
- butcher paper
- crayons
- rulers

Estimation/Measuring/Graphing Snow Pea Pods

The Chinese use snow pea pods in many of the dishes they prepare.

Sorting, Sprouting, Planting Seeds

1. Children fold their papers in horizontal quarters.
2. Give each child a pea pod and have each estimate how many peas are in the pod and record it in the top quarter.
3. Each child measures the length of his or her pod, then records its length and draws it actual size in quarter #2.

4. Tell the children: Open your pod and count the number of peas in it. Record the number of peas in quarter #3. Taste the peas and write how they taste.

5. In quarter #4, draw all the peas in detail.

6. On two class graphs made from butcher paper, record how many peas were in your pods and how long your pods were.

7. After the activity is complete, read the graphs with the children, asking such questions as: How many people had ____ peas in their pod? Most people had ____ peas, etc.

SCIENCE: Small or Cooperative Groups

You Will Need:
- Student Page 64
- potting mix
- transparent tape
- bean sprouts (one per child)
- 5 different types of seeds of varying sizes, shapes

Seeds and the Chinese

Seeds are important sources of food in China. Rice is a seed and the mainstay of the Chinese diet. Rice needs lots of water so the Chinese people grow it in paddies filled with water. Bean sprouts are used a lot in Chinese cooking too. The Chinese also roast watermelon seeds and eat them like we eat sunflower seeds.

1. Mix up all the seeds and give each group of children five paper cups, some potting soil, a small handful of seeds, a bean sprout for each child, and transparent tape.

2. Have the children sort the seeds and record the number of seed types on their papers.

3. Explain how a seed sprouts and point out its different parts. Have the children locate the parts of their bean sprouts, record them, then taste the bean sprouts.

4. Then have them tape one of each kind of seed to the outside of a paper cup (so they will know what plant comes from which seed). Plant the rest of each type of seed in potting soil in the cups. Mark them with the group's name, water them, and record the growth over several days.

Note: Sprouts are fun to grow in glass jars with perforated lids. They can be eaten later.

Student Page 64: Children sort their seeds and record the different types they have. They draw their bean sprouts, identify the parts of the sprout, and taste them. Then they plant their seeds, watch, and record the growth over the next several days.

Note: You may wish to have each group graph the growth of the plants.

SOCIAL STUDIES: Whole Group

You Will Need:
- Student Page 58
- red butcher paper
- construction paper
- several long blankets (for dragon)
- plastic laundry basket w/handles
- scissors
- paste
- paint

Map

Locate the continent of Asia on the map (Student Page 58), then locate China on it. Color China.

Chinese New Year

This traditional celebration is a centuries-old spring festival. The Chinese lunar calendar determines the date so it usually occurs between the middle of January and the middle of February.

1. For the Chinese, the New Year is a time to get rid of the old and welcome the new. If people owe money, they try to pay their debts before the New Year.

2. Families hang scrolls with short poems about good wishes written in Chinese. The family also makes an arrangement of oranges because the Chinese word for orange sounds like the word for "wealth."

3. On New Year's Eve a big family dinner or banquet is served with traditional Chinese food. After dinner, the children stay up late and bow to their elders as a sign of respect. The children receive red envelopes of lucky money called "Lai-See" throughout the New Year. In China, red is the good luck color. Only paper money is given since coins are thought to be bad luck.

4. According to the Chinese Zodiac Calendar, each year is associated with a different animal. Those people born in the year of a certain animal are thought to exhibit certain characteristics.

5. The last day of the Chinese New Year, the Dragon Parade takes place. It is considered the highlight of the whole New Year celebration. The dragon is accompanied by firecrackers to scare away evil spirits and bad luck.

Note: Arrange four oranges as a New Year display—three on the bottom, one on top. Red lucky money envelopes can be found at many Asian food markets. Chinese fortune cookies are not a Chinese tradition; they are an American invention.

To Make A Dragon: Invert the plastic laundry basket, cover it with red butcher paper (leaving holes for the eyes), and decorate it with paint and construction paper to look like the head of a dragon.

For the Dragon Dance, have children line up in single file, arms on the waist of the child in front of them with blankets draped over themselves to form the long, snake-like body of the dragon. The child in the lead holds the dragon's head over himself or herself and leads the parade dance by dramatically dipping and swaying the large head from side to side. The rest of the children follow the leader as they are led in serpentine movements around the classroom and outside.

ART: Whole Group

You Will Need:
- butcher paper (for teacher's example)
- rolls of white shelf paper
- black watercolor paint
- paintbrushes
- Chinese Characters

Chinese Characters

Chinese writing is traditionally done with a brush and black ink on paper. The Chinese don't use an alphabet as we do; they use characters that have meaning by themselves. The words are written from top to bottom. There are thousands of Chinese characters.

1. Cut a length of shelf paper for each child's "scroll."

2. Have children hold their brushes straight up and down without their arms resting on the paper. This is the traditional way to hold the brush.

3. Write numbers 1–10 and other symbols on butcher paper for children to copy.

1 = 一 "i"
2 = 二 "erh"
3 = 三 "san"
4 = 四 "ssu"
5 = 五 "wu"
6 = 六 "liu"
7 = 七 "chi"
8 = 八 "pa"
9 = 九 "chiu"
10 = 十 "shih"

女 = woman
日 = sun
月 = moon
雨 = rain
土 = earth
木 = tree
火 = fire
山 = mountain

Crow Boy

by Taro Yashima

READ ALOUD: Whole Group

Before Reading Activity

How does it feel to be different at school? (Discuss.)

This is a story of a Japanese boy named Chibi. He is different too. Listen to what happens and to what school life is like in Japan.

Teacher Reads Aloud

Crow Boy, by Taro Yashima.

After Reading Activity

What did Chibi do about being different? How is he the same as you? What is school life like in Japan? (Discuss.)

WRITING: Whole Group or Small Groups

Group Activity
Haiku Poems

Haiku poetry is a Japanese invention that paints a picture of nature with words. Haiku has a strict form in Japan but the number of syllables can be relaxed for this exercise. In Japan the poem has 17 syllables in all, consisting of three lines of 5 - 7 - 5 syllables respectively. The imagery uses feelings, questions, and descriptive words to convey the poem. Read Haiku poems to the children to spark their ideas.

Have children dictate lines of haiku poetry that you write on the board. Do several until the class feels comfortable with the concept and can write their own.

Note: The book In the Eyes of the Cat by Demi (Holt, 1992) is filled with haiku poems for children.

Pre-Writers: Copy a poem from the board. Draw a picture to go along with it.

Beginning Writers: Copy the first line of a haiku poem and complete it on your own. Illustrate it.

Experienced Writers: Write your own haiku poems about favorite nature subjects. Illustrate them when you are done.

ACTIVITY CHOICES:

Children choose one or two of these activities to do in a 1- to 1½-hour block of time.

Cooking and Eating with Chopsticks

In both China and Japan, people eat with chopsticks. The Chinese cook in a wok (a rounded metal pan) over high heat. The vegetables are cut into bite-sized pieces and stir-fried very quickly. This method conserves fuel and retains the nutrients in the food.

You Will Need:

- hot plate
- wok (or large fry pan)
- pot w/lid for rice
- cutting board
- 2 Tbsp. oil
- rice
- 8-10 cups cut vegetables
- paper bowls (one per child)
- wooden chopsticks (a set per child)
- sharp knives
- cooking/serving spoon
- ½ cup soy sauce
- 1-3 Tbsp. corn starch
- 2 cups chicken broth

1. Cook rice, following package instructions.
2. While rice is cooking, cut vegetables into bite-sized pieces.
3. Stir-fry vegetables in 2 Tbsp. oil in hot wok or fry pan. Mix 1 Tbsp. corn starch into ½ cup soy sauce. Just before vegetables are done, pour in soy sauce mixture. Serve over rice once sauce is thickened.
4. Children eat vegetables over rice from their bowls with chopsticks.

Origami

Origami is the Japanese art of paper folding. Make a samurai helmet or an airplane by following the directions on Student Page 65.

You Will Need:
- Student Page 65
- 8½" x 11" colored paper or wrapping paper (note: construction paper is too heavy)

European and Asian Games

Many games children play today were imported from Europe and Asia.

You Will Need:
- jacks and/or small pebbles (5 needed for a game)
- checkers and checkerboards
- chalk or tape to mark off hopscotch games

1. Jacks is a game imported from Asia where boys and girls both played it. Instead of using a small ball to bounce, just 5 jacks or small pebbles are used. The child throws one jack in the air, picks one up from the ground and catches the thrown one. This continues until the child misses picking up a jack or catching the one thrown. Other variations involve

picking up two, three, and all four jacks at a time; or catching the jack on the back of the hand.

2. Checkers is a European game. In France it is called "dames." In England it is called "draughts." The pilgrims brought this game with them on the Mayflower, and they named it checkers. Have the children play the regular rules of the game.

3. Hopscotch has a number of variations. It is played in Europe as well as Russia and China. The basic rules have the child hopping on one and both feet through the game, and using a marker (called a "potsie" in Britain) which moves from square to square. One cannot hop in the square where the potsie is. Here are some hopscotch frames to draw:

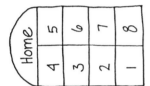 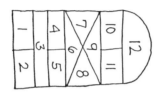  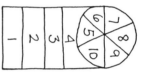

In these games the children toss the potsie into successive numbered squares without its touching the line. Then they hop with either one or both feet into successive numbered squares, making sure not to step on a line or in a square with a potsie.

4. Stone, Scissors, Paper is a Japanese finger game called "janken." Children make a fist to represent the stone "ishi," put out two fingers for scissors "hasami," or flatten their hand to mean paper "kami." Stone conquers scissors because it can bend them, scissors conquer paper since they cut paper, and paper conquers stone because it can cover it.

Note: Other Japanese games include badminton and spinning tops.

SCIENCE: Small or Cooperative Groups

You Will Need:
- frozen fish (one per group)
- newspaper
- paint brush
- black paint or ink
- blank newsprint

Fish Prints
The country of Japan is a series of islands. The nation depends on the sea for much of its food. Therefore, fish are very important to the Japanese. Much of Japanese art involves fish as a subject. Making fish prints is one such art.

1. Fish have gills to get oxygen from the water. Scales cover their bodies. When making a fish print it is important that the gills and scales show well. Do not worry about the eye— Japanese artists draw it in later to give a lifelike quality.

2. Place the fish on newspaper. Paint a very thin layer of black paint on it, then lay a piece of paper over it. Lightly press down without moving the paper, then peel it off. The fish print is complete when the eye is painted in.

SOCIAL STUDIES: Whole, Small or Cooperative Groups

You Will Need:
- Student Page 58
- butcher paper
- marking pens

Map
Locate the continent of Asia on the map (Student Page 58). Find Japan and color it.

Japanese Customs

1. The Japanese celebrate the New Year at a different time than do the Chinese. Families gather together and play a number of games that include badminton ("hanet suki"), spinning tops, and flying kites. It is a time when women wear a traditional long dress called a kimono.

2. A doll festival called "Hina Matsuri" occurs March 3. On this day girls in Japan set up a display of special dolls. The dolls usually include a prince and princess, warriors, and musicians and are set up in an atmosphere of lanterns, spring flowers, and special pounded rice cakes called "mochi."

   Note: Both boys and girls in the class can bring a favorite doll to place in a Hina Matsuri scene set up in the classroom. Each child can share the significance of his or her doll.

My Grandma Lived In Gooligulch

by Graeme Base

READ ALOUD: Whole Group

Before Reading Activity

What is your grandmother like? Where does she live? Does she have any funny habits or things she does? (Discuss.)

This story is about a grandma who lives in a place called Gooligulch in Australia. Listen to what it's like to live in her house.

Teacher Reads Aloud

My Grandma Lived in Gooligulch, by Graeme Base.

After Reading Activity

What was this grandma like? How was she the same as and different from your Grandma? (Discuss.)

WRITING: Whole Group or Small Groups

Group Activity

Poem: Discuss special and funny things about children's own grandmothers—their habits, pets, etc. List them on the board, then model writing a four-line rhyming poem from information.

Pre-Writers: Copy poem from board. Draw a picture about your grandmother.

Beginning Writers: Make up a poem about your grandmother. Draw a picture to go with it.

Experienced Writers: Write a poem about your grandmother (preferably one longer than four lines). Illustrate your work when done.

READING EXPERIENCE: Whole Group, Small or Cooperative Groups, Pairs

You Will Need:
- paper
- pencils
- crayons

Drawing Conclusions

Discuss what might have happened to Grandma after the end of the story. "Chain" responses on the board.

Example:

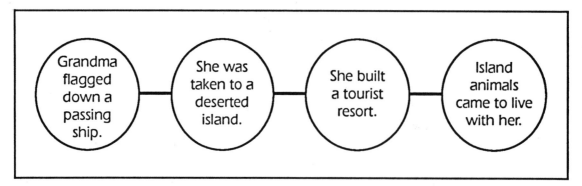

Student Assignment: Students draw and write a chain of events they think happened after the end of the story. (Note: Pre-writers just draw a chain of pictures and tell their stories to a partner or adult.)

MATH: Whole Group or Small Groups

You Will Need:
- Student Page 66
- pencils
- crayons

Great Barrier Reef Calculations

The Great Barrier Reef is the longest coral reef in the world, running 2,000 kilometers along the northeast coast of Australia. The reef supports a wide range of sea life.

Student Page 66: Children follow the directions and color marine animals. Then they work the problems and write down the answers.

SCIENCE: Whole Group

You Will Need:
- Student Page 67
- 9" x 12" white construction paper (one per child)
- scissors
- crayons
- paste

Triarama: Australia's Animals

Because Australia is a continent unattached to any other land mass, its animals are unique and live nowhere else in the world. Many of them are marsupials, meaning their young are born in a premature state and are suckled in a pouch until they mature enough to fend for themselves.

1. **Duckbilled Platypus**—a strange looking creature. Its body is covered with fur, its feet are webbed, and it has a leather-like bill that looks like a duck. Though it lays eggs, the babies are suckled after they hatch.

2. **Kangaroo**—a marsupial. There are fifty-eight different kinds of kangaroos. They live on the ground and hop to get around. A young kangaroo is called a joey and can be seen being carried in its mother's pouch when it is quite big.

3. **Wombat**—similar to a koala but lives on the ground. They eat grass and burrow into the ground.

4. **Koala**—a marsupial that lives in eucalyptus trees and eats only eucalyptus leaves. Once a koala's babies leave the pouch, they are carried on their mother's back.

5. **Emu**—a large bird that can't fly but can run very fast. It looks much like an ostrich. Emu eggs are the size of softballs, and the father hatches the eggs and rears the chicks.

Student Page 67: Children color the animals, cut them out, and follow directions for making the triarama.

SOCIAL STUDIES: Whole Group

You Will Need:
- Student Page 58
- crayons

Map
Locate Australia on the map (Student Page 58). Color it.

Aborigines
The story of Australia's Aborigines is similar to the history of Native Americans. The Aborigines are the native people of Australia. The name "Aborigine" came from Latin, meaning "from the very first."

1. Aboriginal culture is tied to the land. They believe every part of the land is living and is inhabited by spirits who created the world, in a time in the past called "Dreamtime."

2. They are nomadic people and carry tools that serve many purposes. One of those tools is the boomerang. It is used for killing birds and chasing animals into traps. The boomerang is also used as an earth scraper, fire poker, hole digger, or to create friction when making a fire.

3. Art was and is very important to the Aborigines. Paintings are done on rocks, in caves, and on bark. Many paintings are part of their rituals.

4. A "walkabout" is a journey with a spiritual meaning. There are sacred ancient pathways for people to travel on their walkabout. A walkabout helps Aborigines hear their spiritual messages from Dreamtime.

5. The Aborigines dance their "dreamings" by forming a circle and moving in short steps, stamping their feet in rhythm.

Dream Dancing

Children form a circle. Instruct them to think of dreams or happy memories they had. Together they move around the circle, taking small steps and stamping their feet in unison to a rhythm. (For example: loud, soft, soft, soft, loud, loud, soft, soft and repeat.) They can wave their arms to imitate the dream or happy memory, but the most important thing is to hold the thought in mind while dancing.

ART: Whole Group

You Will Need:
- Student Page 68
- colored pens
- crayons

Aboriginal Art

On rocks, caves, bark, and now on canvas, Aborigines draw beautifully stylized pictures of the animals around them. They decorate them with colorful, intricate geometric designs.

Student Page 68: Children use crayons and colored pens to color the designs and decorate the pictures. The lizard picture is the only one fully decorated. Encourage children to decorate the others with geometric lines and dots.

On The Pampas

by Maria Cristina Brusca

READ ALOUD: Whole Group

Before Reading Activity

What would it be like to be on a cowboy ranch all summer long?

This story is about a ranch in South America in a country called Argentina. They have cowboys known as gauchos. Listen for how they are the same as and different from cowboys.

Teacher Reads Aloud

On the Pampas, by Maria Cristina Brusca.

After Reading Activity

How are cowboys and gauchos the same and different? (List on board.)

WRITING: Whole Group or Small Groups

Group Activity

Similarities/Differences: Discuss the list generated in the After Reading Activity. Model writing sentences from list.

Pre-Writers: Copy a sentence from the board. Draw a picture to go with it.

Beginning Writers: Write about how cowboys and gauchos are the same and how they are different. Draw pictures to go with them.

Experienced Writers: Write at least two ways cowboys and gauchos are alike and how they are different. Illustrate your work when done.

READING EXPERIENCE: Whole Group, Small or Cooperative Groups

You Will Need:
- Student Page 69
- pencils
- crayons
- scissors

Fold Book: Vacation Album

This activity is meant to encourage children to take on the character's point of view in the story On the Pampas.

Before Reading Activity

Pretend you are the character in the story, listen to the story, and think about what three of your favorite things on the pampas would have been.

Read On the Pampas, by Maria Cristina Brusca.

After Reading Activity

What were some of the things you would have liked on the pampas? (List on board.)

Student Page 69: Ask students to recall details of the story and to draw and write about what their favorite experiences on the pampas would have been.

MATH: Whole Group, Small or Cooperative Groups

You Will Need:
- Student Page 70   • pencils   • crayons

Map Reading

South America is a large continent with flat grasslands (the pampas), high mountains, popular beaches, and dense rain forests.

Student Page 70: Follow the directions regarding the map, then answer the questions. It is best for the teacher to work through the page with the children since it is more important to read the map than to check for wrong answers.

SCIENCE: Whole Group or Small Groups

You Will Need:
- butcher paper   • crayons   • scissors   • magazines   • paste

The Rain Forests

A large portion of the earth's rain forests are located in South America, and these special woodlands are being destroyed.

1. Rain forests get a lot of rain. In fact, it rains almost every day in the rain forest. The trees and plants turn much of the water back into the air so it can rain somewhere else.

2. The trees and plants also make lots of oxygen that goes into the earth's atmosphere. People need that oxygen to breathe and to live.

3. The trees and plants are being cut down for wood and to make places for mining metal, raising cattle, and building houses.

4. The Indians of the rain forest have learned to use the plants and animals of the forest and to live in harmony with them. Many of our modern medicines come from plants in the rain forest. There could be many other medicine-producing plants there, too, but if the rain forests are destroyed, we won't know about them.

5. Foods and other things we use a lot come from the rain forest. Chocolate comes from the cocoa plant grown in the rain forest. Many things are made from rubber, and rubber trees grow in the rain forest.

Tapioca, sometimes made into pudding and used to thicken sauces, is a rain forest plant. So are Brazil nuts, cashews, bananas, mangos, and papayas.

6. One way to help the rain forest is to buy food that grows there, especially bananas and nuts. Another way to help is not to buy things made of wood from the rain forests.

Student Assignment: Discuss products in which rubber, chocolate, nuts, and bananas are used (e.g. rubber—tennis shoes, tires, balls, erasers, etc.). Working in small groups, children cut pictures from magazines of foods and items derived from rain forest products. Paste and label them on butcher paper. Share results with class.

SOCIAL STUDIES: Whole Group

You Will Need:
- Student Page 58
- crayons
- pencils
- white construction paper

Map
Locate South America on the map (Student Page 58). Color it.

Save the Rain Forests Poster
On white construction paper, children make posters about saving the rain forests.

ART: Whole Group

You Will Need:
- Student Page 71
- scissors
- crayons
- paste
- yarn (2½ feet per child)
- red lipstick (optional)

39

Amazon Headdress

Tribes living in the rain forest along the Amazon wear crowns of bright feathers from parrots and macaws. They don these for ceremonies and mark their faces and bodies with red paint.

Student Page 71:

1. Children color and cut out the headband. Then paste the long feathers on the front.

2. Fold the marked edge of the band. Lay yarn along the crease. Paste it shut.

3. To wear feather crown, tie it around the head.

A dance can be performed by children, forming a line with each child putting his or her left arm on the right shoulder of the person ahead. In rhythm, everyone takes a large step and bounces, then takes another and bounces. The leader leads the class in a random serpentine. This dance celebrates a successful harvest.

Optional: Children put stripes on their faces with red lipstick.

Mufaro's Beautiful Daughters

by John Steptoe

READ ALOUD: Whole Group

Before Reading Activity

This story is about two daughters in Africa who live in a country called Zimbabwe. Listen to the story and look at the illustrations to find out as many things as you can about Zimbabwe.

Teacher Reads Aloud

Mufaro's Beautiful Daughters, by John Steptoe.

After Reading Activity

What can you tell about Zimbabwe from the story? (Discuss and list on board.)

WRITING: Whole, Small or Cooperative Groups

Group Activity

Research and Expository Writing: Take the list generated during the After Reading Activity. Model further research using the encyclopedia or other reference material to learn more. Have children dictate sentences using all the information. Write their sentences on the board.

Pre-Writers: Draw a picture and copy a sentence from the board.

Beginning Writers: Draw and write a sentence or two about Zimbabwe.

Experienced Writers: Write a paragraph about Zimbabwe. Illustrate it.

READING EXPERIENCE: Small or Cooperative Groups, Pairs

You Will Need:
- one picture book per child (use their library books)

Research

This activity acquaints children with the process of researching or finding out information in an enjoyable way.

1. In pairs or small groups, children look carefully through their picture books to gain information.

2. They explain to their partner or group about the setting of the story and share the pictures and the process of how they arrived at their conclusions.

MATH: Whole Group or Small Groups

You Will Need:
- Student Page 72   - pencils

Hieroglyphic Code

Africa is the second largest continent. It has many different countries with different histories and customs. One of the most fascinating is the culture of ancient Egypt. More than 4,000 years ago the Egyptians invented a type of writing called hieroglyphics—picture writing that stood for sounds. A person's name was written in an oval with a line underneath it. This configuration is called a "cartouche."

Student Page 72: Children work out the code of the hieroglyphics, then write their names in the cartouche.

SCIENCE: Whole Group or Small Groups

You Will Need:
- 9" x 12" white construction paper   • crayons   • pencils

African Animal Mix-up

This activity uses children's knowledge of African animals and applies it in an enjoyable, unique way.

1. Discuss African animals with the class. Generate a list of animals on the board.

2. Discuss animal attributes— markings, coverings (fur or skin), trunks, spots, etc.— and what their heads, bodies, and feet look like.

3. Have each child fold a piece of construction paper in thirds. (For young ones, you may wish to do this for them ahead of time.) Arrange the paper in an accordion fold.

4. Each child draws and colors the head of an African animal on the top third, folds it so only the second third shows, and passes it to another child. The new child draws and colors the body of an African animal on the second third, folds the paper so only the last third shows, and passes it on. The legs and feet are the last pictures drawn and colored on the final third.

5. Once head, body, legs/feet are complete, children open up their mixed-up animal picture and name it based on the parts of animals represented.

6. In pairs or small groups, children explain what their animals eat and other special things about them.

SOCIAL STUDIES: Whole Group

You Will Need:
- Student Page 58
- crayons
- pencils
- white construction paper

Map

Locate Africa and the countries of Zimbabwe, Egypt, and Ghana (Student Page 58). Color them.

Egypt/Ghana and Swahili

These three activities cover North, East, and West Africa, providing a good cross-section of cultures, climate, and history.

1. Egypt is in the northwest part of Africa. Most of North Africa is a desert called the Sahara, but most of the people in Egypt live along the Nile River. They can grow crops along the banks of the river.

   Egypt has a history dating back more than 5,000 years. The rulers of ancient Egypt were called pharaohs. They built great pyramids out of stone blocks that were much bigger and heavier than a grown person.

   In ancient Egypt, the people believed the body had to be preserved after death, so they made mummies. It took seventy days to make a mummy because there were many steps in the process. The body was carefully wrapped with bandages and put in a coffin. After the mummy was put in the tomb, Egyptians believed the soul, or "ka," of the dead person moved about between the spirit and real world.

2. Ghana is on the West African coast. Part of Ghana is covered by dense jungles, other parts by grasslands. Cocoa, coffee, rubber, and rice are the main crops grown in Ghana. The people wear bright-colored cloths with beautiful designs, wrapped around them like robes. A tradition of painting bold designs on cotton with a stick is still practiced today.

   Ghana has always had a rich history, but things turned bad when Europeans started the slave trade. Many people were taken in chains from all parts of West Africa and put on slave ships bound across the sea. Many Africans died before they reached their destination. The slave trade was finally stopped.

3. Swahili is a language spoken in East Africa. It developed as a trade language so people exchanging goods in the region from East Africa to Zambia and the Congo and even as far as Pakistan could speak a common tongue and be understood.

   Listed are some Swahili words, their meanings, and pronunciations. Have children practice using them.

Africa

- baba (bah-bah) = father
- chakula (cha-koo-lah) = food
- jambo (jahm-bow) = hello
- karibu (kah-ree-boo) = welcome
  When someone asks, "Hodi?" (May I come in?), the answer is karibu.
- mama (mah-mah) = mother
- ngoma (n-go-mah) = drum and dance
- rafiki (rah-fee-key) = friend
- shule (shoe-lay) = school
- watoto (wah-toe-toe) = children

ART: Whole Group

You Will Need:
- coffee cans with plastic lids
- round oatmeal boxes
- toilet paper tubes
- construction paper
- white copy paper
- crayons
- scissors
- paste
- dry beans

Drums, Rattles, Chants

Every African nation, native or otherwise, uses drums and other percussion instruments for celebrations and holidays.

Drums: Cover coffee cans and oatmeal boxes with construction paper that has been decorated. (Remind children of Egyptian hieroglyphics and Ghana designs already studied.) Cover with lids. Hold under one arm and play them with hands or curved sticks.

Insert beans

Rattles: Put a few dry beans in toilet paper tubes. Paste over the ends with rounds of white ditto/copy paper. Then wrap tube with decorated construction paper.

Cover ends

Wrap with decorated paper

Chants: Denko is a chant accompanied by drums and rattles. Denko means "to have a child." The lyrics are about all the things a mother does to look after the welfare of her children.

> Denko et denko ye
> Mousoo lou ye ne na koun ye
> Denko et denko ye
> Tieba i kan son dola

Another chant accompanies a children's game in Ghana called "Kye Kye Kule." The leader places his or her hands on head and sings "Kye, Kye, Kule." The other players do the same thing and repeat the words. Next, the leader puts hands on shoulders and sings, "Kye, Kye, Kule," and the players do the same. This continues until the leader gets down to his/her toes, then falls down. When everyone else falls down, the leader jumps up without warning and tries to tag one of the players. However, the players can't run until the leader runs. The person who is tagged becomes the leader.

Once A Mouse

by Marcia Brown

READ ALOUD: Whole Group

Before Reading Activity
This is a story that takes place in India. Watch for animals that live there.

Teacher Reads Aloud
Once a Mouse, by Marcia Brown.

After Reading Activity
What animals were in the story and live in India? (Discuss.)

WRITING: Whole Group or Small Groups

Group Activity
Chart Story: Ask the children what they can tell about tigers from the story. List the information on the board. Then tell them more about tigers, and write a chart story dictated by the students.

Example: Tigers live in forests or grassy areas. They live by themselves and don't travel in groups. Orange with black stripes, they prey on deer, cattle, and other animals. Tigers in India are called Bengal tigers.

Pre-Writers: Copy a sentence from the chart story. Draw a picture about it.

Beginning Writers: Draw and write a sentence or two about tigers.

Experienced Writers: Write your own paragraph about tigers. Illustrate your work.

READING EXPERIENCE: Whole Group, Small or Cooperative Groups

You Will Need:
- Student Page 73
- book: Once a Mouse, by Marcia Brown
- crayons
- scissors
- paste

Sequencing Story Events
Before Reading Activity: What happened in the story? (Draw/write events on board.) Listen carefully to the order in which the events happened in the story.

Teacher Reads Aloud: Once a Mouse, by Marcia Brown.

After Reading Activity: What happened first in the story? What happened next, etc.? (Order events on the board according to student responses.)

Student Page 73: Children color, cut, and paste the events of the story in proper order.

MATH: Whole Group or Small Groups

You Will Need:
- Student Page 74   ▪ crayons   ▪ scissors   ▪ paste

Discrimination: The Taj Mahal

The Taj Mahal is a temple built by a prince in memory of his dead wife. Its great white domes are made of white stone. The Taj Mahal is a beautiful sight.

Student Page 74: Children cut and paste the pieces to re-create the Taj Mahal on their paper.

SCIENCE: Whole Group or Small Groups

You Will Need:
- white construction paper   ▪ crayons   ▪ pencils

The Himalayas

The Himalaya Mountains are the tallest mountain range in the world. There are many high peaks in the Himalayas. In India the highest peak is Kanchenjunga. Nepal, a country bordering India, is where the highest peak in the world stands—Mt. Everest.

1. The Himalayas are covered with snow year-round.

2. Some people believe a creature called the Yeti lives high in the snow-covered Himalayas. They think the Yeti is taller than a man, covered with white fur, and has very big feet.

3. People who climb the Himalayas have to use very special equipment and warm clothes, special boots, food, tents, cameras, rope, ice axes, etc.

4. One of the dangers climbers face is an avalanche. That is when lots of snow breaks loose and slides down the mountain. An avalanche can bury climbers.

Student Assignment: Children fold their paper in half. On one half they draw the Himalayas and what they think a Yeti looks like. On the other half they draw all the things they would pack to climb the Himalayas.

SOCIAL STUDIES: Whole Group

You Will Need:
- Student Page 58
- crayons
- pencils
- Map

Locate India on the map (Student Page 58) and color it. Color the rest of Asia too.

Hindu Festivals

Over 80 percent of India's population is Hindu. The festivals Hindu people celebrate are linked with the seasons as well as with specific gods.

1. The two main Hindu festivals are Divali and Holi.

2. Divali is an autumn festival celebrated with lights. It is the most exciting holiday of the year for Hindu children. Most of the day is spent making "diyas"—special lamps for the festival. Gifts are exchanged, and fairs have exciting rides and fireworks. It is believed that all the lights will guide the goddess of wealth and fortune down to earth on her heavenly swan, to bless people with wealth and good luck.

3. Holi is a springtime festival dedicated to one of the gods called Krishna. People throw bright-colored powder on each other in the street. At the end of the day, everyone's clothes are splashed with bright colors.

4. Swings are set up and decorated for the spring festival. The Hindus believe the higher people can swing, the closer they get to the gods.

5. Dancing is very important to the Hindus. Special temple dancers perform at festivals. They dress in elaborate costumes and can tell whole stories just by the way they hold their hands, neck, and eyes. Hindus believe that one of the main gods named Shiva danced to bring order to the universe.

Compare and contrast the Indian holidays of Divali and Holi to Christmas/ Hanukkah and Easter/Passover.

Teach children some of the Indian hand positions called "mudras." Have them move their necks from side to side without moving their shoulders, and hold their eyes wide while looking far to the left then far to the right.

Deer or Cow   World   Love   Bird   Budding Lotus   War

ART: Whole Group

You Will Need:

- Student Page 75
- tagboard
- colored construction paper
- brass brads
- crayons
- colored felt tip pens
- large cardboard box
- white butcher paper
- tape or paper clips
- bright light
- paper punch
- plastic drinking straws

Shadow Puppets

Shadow puppets are an ancient Indian form of entertainment.

Student Page 75:

1. Make templates of tagboard.

2. Have children trace around templates of the characters they choose on colored construction paper.

3. They draw features on the characters with colored felt tip pens. (Note: the construction paper will cast a shadow and show features the children have drawn.)

4. Fix the puppets together with brads.

5. Attach straws as handles for the moving parts, using brads. Punch a hole through the end of the straw with a hole punch and attach it with a brad to the puppet.

6. Children perform shadow puppet shows of <u>Once a Mouse</u> and other stories they might make up with the characters.

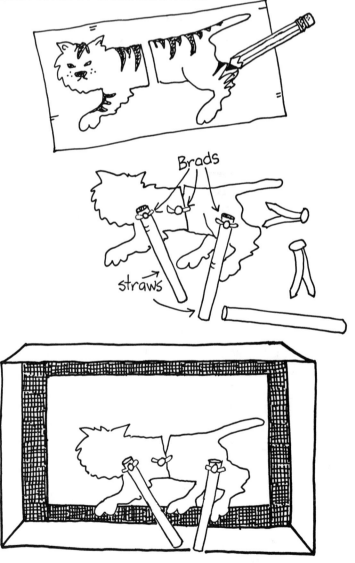

To make a shadow puppet theater, cut a large rectangle out of the bottom of the box, leaving a two-inch frame around it. Leave the top open. Cover the bottom and sides of the box with butcher paper or screen material.

Where The Children Live

by Thomas B. Allen

READ ALOUD: Whole Group

Before Reading Activity

What kinds of houses do children around the world live in? (Discuss and list on board.)

This book tells about the different houses children live in. Look for houses in this book to add to our list.

Teacher Reads Aloud

Where The Children Live, by Thomas B. Allen.

After Reading Activity

What are some of the other houses mentioned in the book? List on board and discuss similarities and differences between them.

Note: Where The Children Live can be used as a springboard into other studies of children around the world.

WRITING: Whole Group or Small Groups

Group Activity

Semantic Mapping: Listen to descriptions of the children and their homes again. (Read a few pages from book.) How would you describe yourself and your house? (Make a small semantic map of student responses on board.)

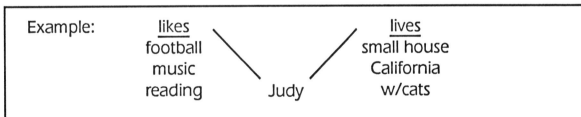

Example: likes   lives
             football   small house
             music   California
             reading   Judy   w/cats

Judy lives in a small house with her cats in California. She likes football, listening to music, and reading.

Pre-Writers: Draw a picture of yourself and the house in which you live. Copy and complete the sentences: "(name) lives in a house in (city). (He/She) likes _____."

Beginning Writers: Draw and write about the house you live in and what you like to do.

Experienced Writers: Write a short paragraph about the house you live in and the things you like to do. Illustrate your work.

ACTIVITY CHOICES:

Children choose one or more of these activities to do in a 1- to 1½-hour block of time.

Dioramas

Construct dioramas of scenes from countries studied throughout the unit.

You Will Need:

- shoeboxes
- construction paper
- paste
- crayons
- scissors
- pipe cleaners

Children draw, cut, and paste a scene from a country. They should be prepared to share their work this afternoon during the art show.

Flags

Each country has its own flag.

You Will Need:

- Student Page 76
- construction paper
- paste
- crayons
- scissors

1. Children follow directions and color the flags on Student Page 76.

2. Once done, each child constructs his or her own flag from construction paper. It can be either a country's flag or an original design.

Curry

Curry is a traditional Indian dish. It is served over rice with condiments added.

You Will Need:

- 8 cups cooked diced chicken
- 8 Tbsp. cooking oil
- 8 large onions, chopped
- 8 large tart apples, chopped
- cooked rice (for whole class)
- 4 tsps. curry powder
- 2-3 Tbsp. cornstarch
- 6 chicken bouillon cubes
- 6 cups stewed tomatoes
- 6 cups hot water
- 5 cups raisins
- 5 cups peanuts
- 2 pkg. shredded coconut
- paper bowls, plastic spoons
- large cooking pot
- sharp knives
- cutting board
- cooking/serving spoons
- hot plate
- ½ cup brown sugar

1. Sauté apples and onions in cooking oil until tender.
2. Dissolve chicken bouillon cubes in hot water and add to apple/onion mixture. Add chicken, stewed tomatoes, brown sugar, and curry powder. Bring to a boil.
3. Dissolve cornstarch in ¼ cup cold water and add to curry. Stir until thickened.
4. During the afternoon Science Activity, serve over rice with raisins, peanuts, and coconut as condiments children add on top of their curry. Enjoy!

Act Out Stories, Songs, Poems, and Dances

Help children recall stories, puppet shows, songs, and dances learned throughout the unit.

You Will Need:
- Amazon dance (Teacher Page 40)
- African chants (Teacher Page 44)
- Aboriginal dance (Teacher Page 36)
- Indian dance (Teacher Page 47)

1. Children rehearse songs and dances learned throughout the unit.
2. They also re-create their haiku poems, act out and pantomime stories read throughout the unit, and even make up their own stories.
3. They should be ready to perform them this afternoon as part of the culminating Art Activity.

CULMINATING ACTIVITIES

SCIENCE: Whole Group

You Will Need:
- 12"x 18" white construction paper
- crayons
- colored pens

Poster

Children make up a poster of all the things they've learned throughout the unit. Encourage them to include art projects, dancing, cooking, and other activities.

Enjoy Curry

Serve and enjoy the curry and condiments made this morning.

SOCIAL STUDIES: Whole Group

You Will Need:
- Student Page 58
- pencils
- stapler
- crayons
- construction paper
- Map

Map

Find all the places mentioned in the book <u>Where The Children Live</u> on Student Page 58. Write and color them.

The places mentioned were:

Nicaragua	Burma	Turkey	Tahiti
Lapland	Tennessee	Ireland	
Netherlands	Maine	Arabia	
Siberia	Arctic lands (Eskimos)	Peru	

Unit Folder

Make a folder of construction paper for holding all the unit's work. Staple the edges when complete.

ART: Whole Group

You Will Need:
- samples of the unit's projects
- costumes children wear for performance

Perform Stories, Songs, Poems, and Dances

In costumes created from projects throughout this unit, children perform all the stories, songs, poems, and dances they practiced for Activity Choices this morning.

Art Show of Unit Projects

Display samples of student work done throughout the unit. This can be done on cardboard panels cut from a refrigerator box as well as on tables, desks, and bulletin boards around the room.

Invite other classrooms, parents, and school officials to join in the class celebration and assign child "ambassadors" to explain the unit and all the projects.

Telling Time

Cut out the clocks at the bottom and paste them in the right place.

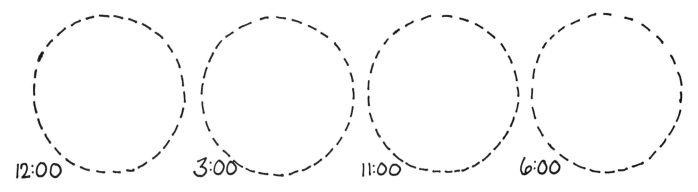

12:00   3:00   11:00   6:00

What time is it?

_____   _____   _____   _____

Think time: Use this clock to answer the questions:

1. What time is it? _____.

2. In 2 hours it will be _____.

3. In 4 hours it will be _____.

4. In China it is 7 hours later. What time is it there? _____

5. In Africa it is 3 hours later. What time is it there? _____

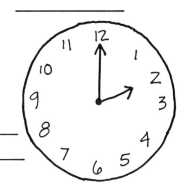

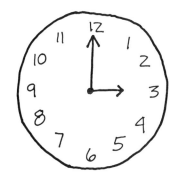   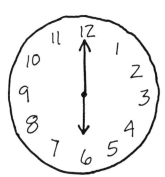

The Continents

There are seven continents on the earth. People live on six of them. People don't live in Antarctica because it is so cold.

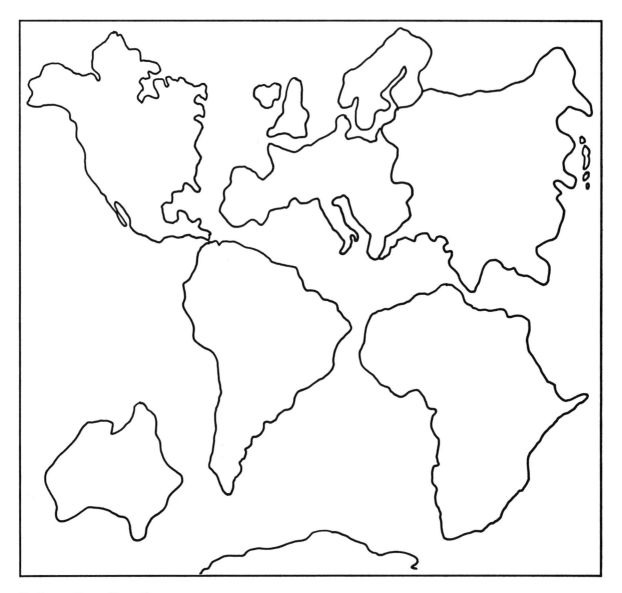

Follow the directions:

1. Color North America yellow.
2. Color South America orange.
3. Color Europe green.
4. Color Africa purple.
5. Color Asia red.

6. Color Australia brown.
7. Leave Antarctica white.
8. Color the oceans blue.
9. Draw a black line along the equator.

Name _____

Flags of North America

Here are the flags of the three largest countries in North America.

CANADA

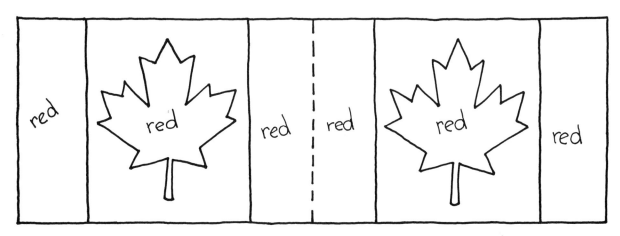

UNITED STATES

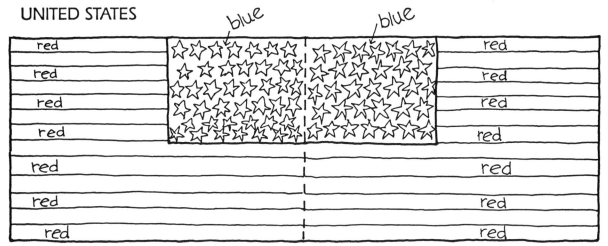

MEXICO

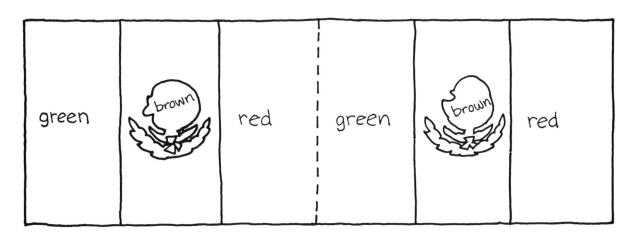

Name _____

British and American Words

British Words		American Words
biscuit	=	cookie
crisps	=	potato chips
chips	=	French fries
chemist	=	drugstore
holiday	=	vacation
lift	=	elevator
torch	=	flashlight
petrol	=	gas
football	=	soccer
headmaster	=	school principal

Write the British name under each picture.

_____   _____   _____

_____

_____   _____   _____

Name _____

Compute-and-Color British Flag

Color all 5's red.
Color all 7's blue.

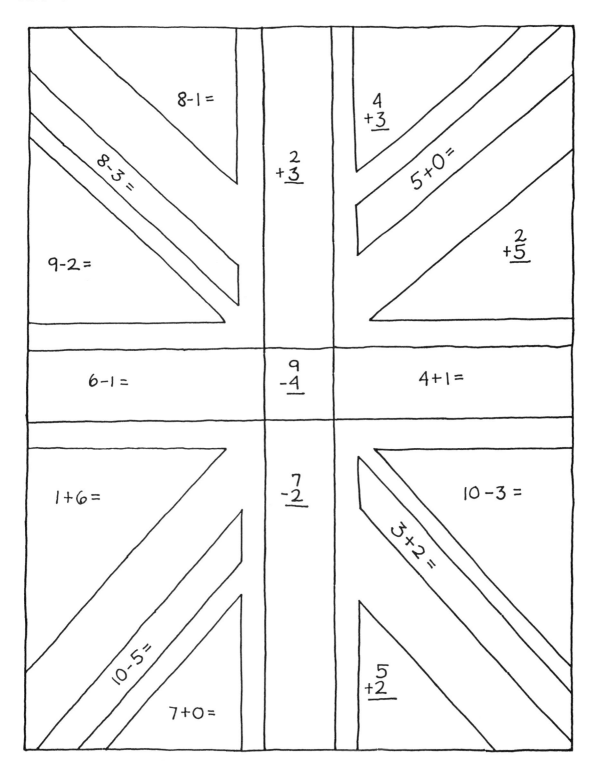

Map

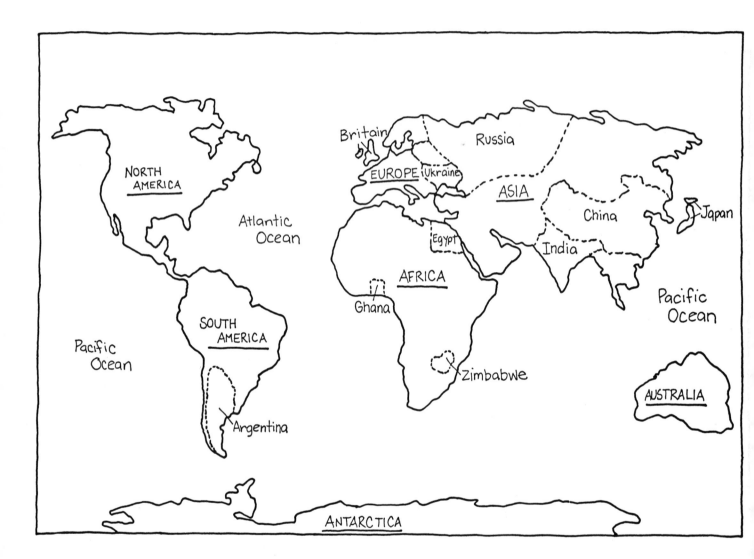

Tower of London

Color, cut, and paste together the Tower and figures below.

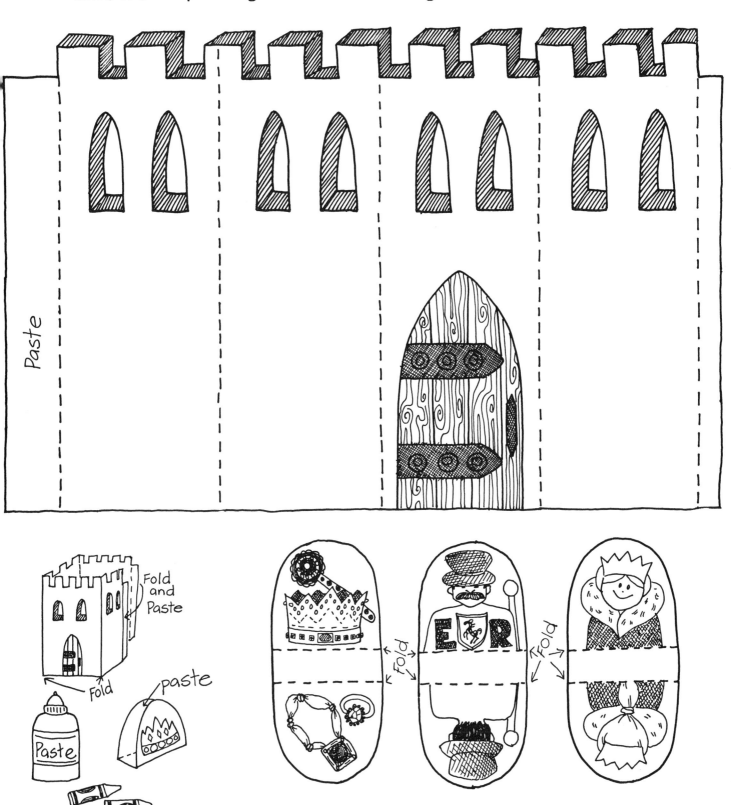

Dialogue Between
Babushka And The Goose

Write what you think Babushka and the goose might say to each other.

Summarizing/Finger Puppets

Color and cut out the puppets. Fold and paste Babushka and the goose together.

Patterning Puzzles

1. Finish drawing the patterns on these eggs. Color them.

2. Cut out the pieces on the bottom and paste them in the right place. Color it when you are done.

3. Color the nesting dolls. Cut them out. Arrange largest to smallest.

Parts Of An Egg

Follow the directions and color the parts of an egg.

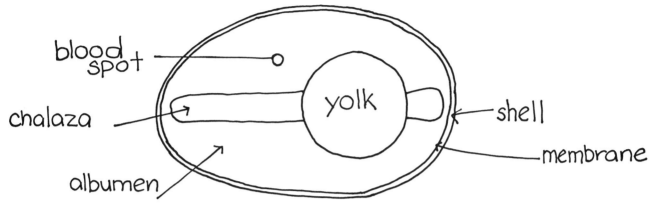

1. Color the yolk orange.
2. Color the blood spot red.
3. Color the albumen yellow.

Draw what the egg looks like in the glass bowl. Draw a line from the word to each part.

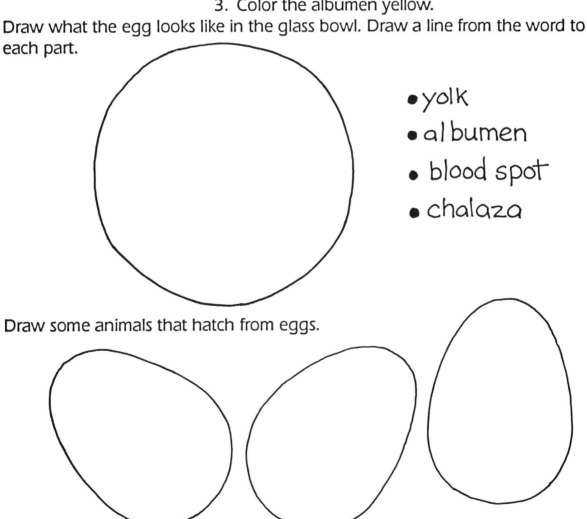

- yolk
- albumen
- blood spot
- chalaza

Draw some animals that hatch from eggs.

Sorting, Sprouting, Planting Seeds

1. Sort your seeds. How many kinds of seeds do you have? _____

2. Draw the different seeds you have.

3. Here are the different parts of a bean sprout. Draw your bean sprout. Find the parts.

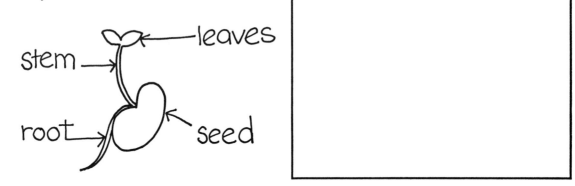

4. Taste your bean sprout. What did it taste like? _____

   _____

   _____

5. Tape a different kind of seed to the outside of each cup. Draw the seed taped to each cup. Draw the plant you think will grow.

6. Put potting soil in each cup. Plant the seeds in the right cup. Water it. Put it in the window.

Name _____

Origami

Follow the pictured instructions to make a samurai helmet or an airplane.

Samurai helmet:

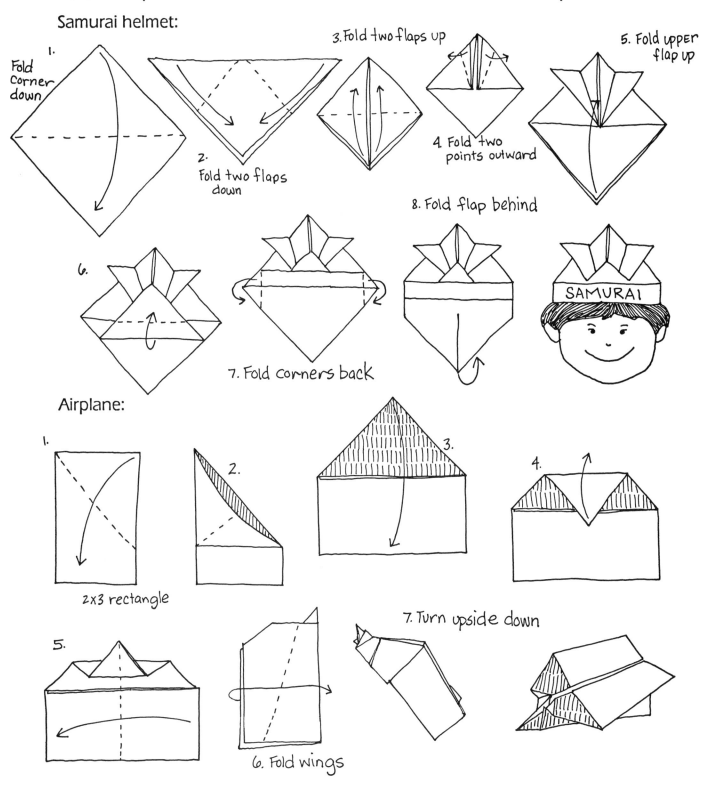

Airplane:

Great Barrier Reef Calculations

Color orange. Color purple.

Color black. Color red.

Color yellow. Color green.

How many ⭐s? _____   How many ⭐ + 🐟 + 🐚? _____

How many 🦈 + 🐟? _____

How many 🐌 + 🐚? _____

How many 🐍? _____

Name _____

Triarama: Australia's Animals

Color the animals and the triarama. Cut them out. Paste the triarama together.
Then paste the animals on the triarama.

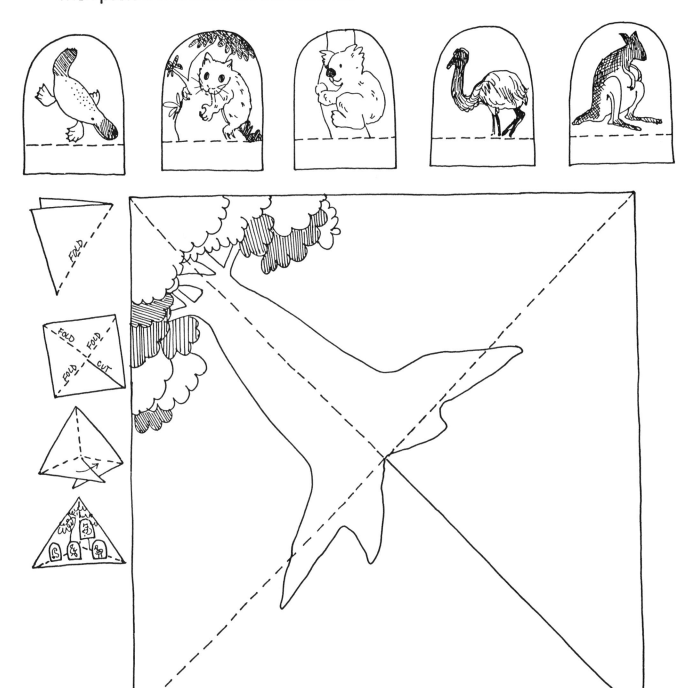

Aboriginal Art

Color the pictures and make more designs on them.

Fold Book: Vacation Album

Cut out and fold the book. Draw pictures and write about your vacation on the pampas.

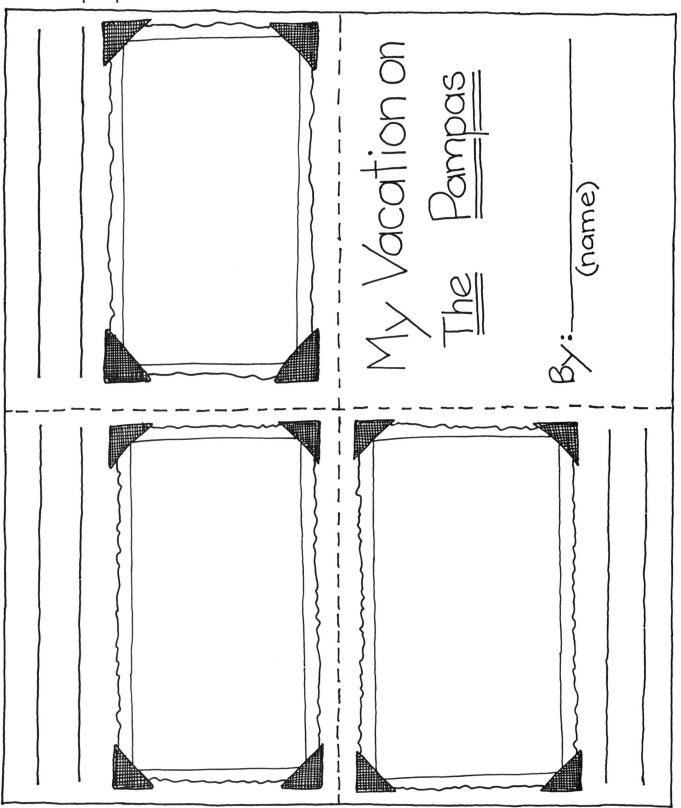

Map Reading

Follow the directions for the map. Then answer the questions.

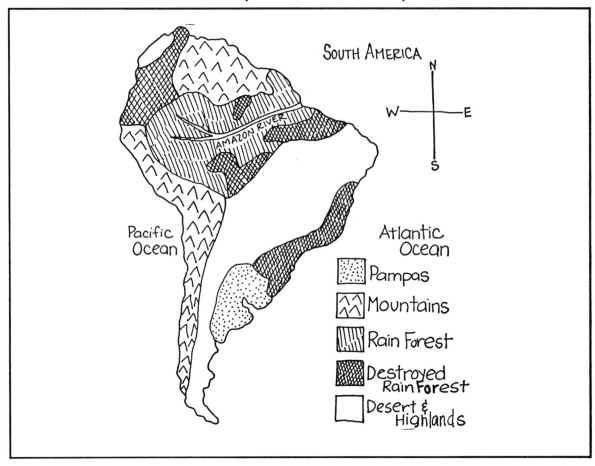

Color ⬚ orange. It is the pampas. Cows and sheep live there.
Color ⬚ brown. They are mountains. The Inca Indians lived there.
Color ⬚ green. It is the rain forest. The Amazon River is there.
Color ⬚ yellow. It is the destroyed rain forest.
Color the Pacific and Atlantic oceans blue.

1. What is ⬚ ? _____.

2. What is ⬚ ? _____.

3. How many places have destroyed rain forests? _____.

4. What river is in the rain forest? _____.

5. What ocean is west of South America? _____.

Think of other questions. Write them on the back of this page.

Name _____

Amazon Headdress

Color and cut out the headdress. Paste the tall feathers on the front. Tie it around your head with yarn.

Paste feathers here!

Hieroglyphic Code

Use the key to solve the code.

Write your name in the cartouche with hieroglyphics.

Name _____

Sequencing Story Events

Color and cut out the pictures at the bottom of the page. Paste them in the right order.

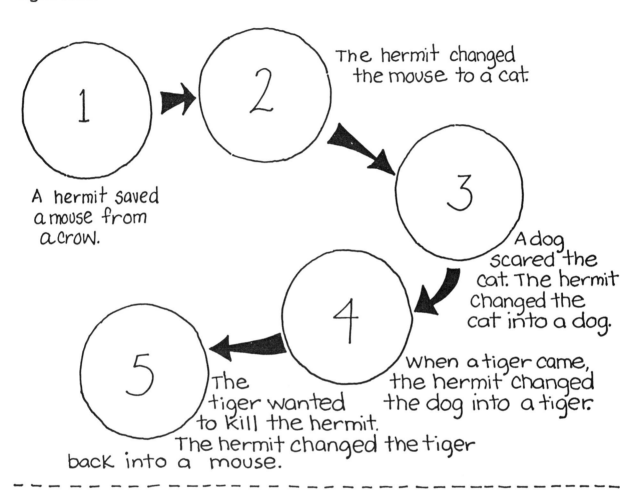

1

2 The hermit changed the mouse to a cat.

A hermit saved a mouse from a crow.

3 A dog scared the cat. The hermit changed the cat into a dog.

4 When a tiger came, the hermit changed the dog into a tiger.

5 The tiger wanted to kill the hermit. The hermit changed the tiger back into a mouse.

73

Discrimination: The Taj Mahal

Cut out the pieces on the bottom and paste them in the box to look like the top picture.

Shadow Puppets

Brads

Flags

Color the flags.

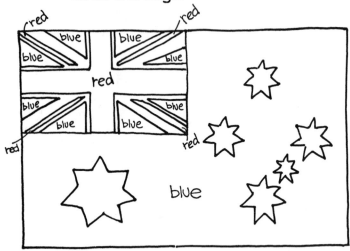

AUSTRALIA

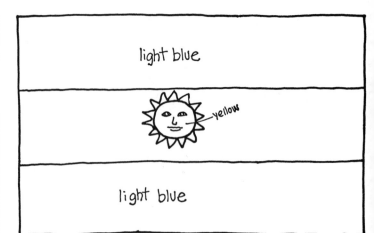

ARGENTINA

CHINA

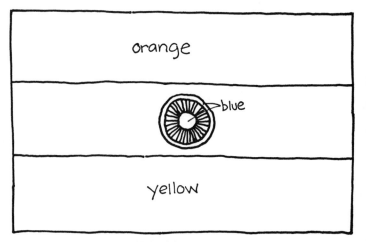

INDIA

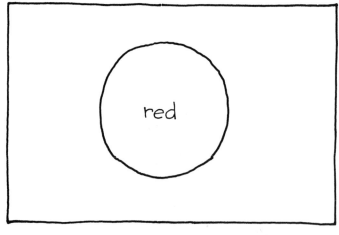

JAPAN

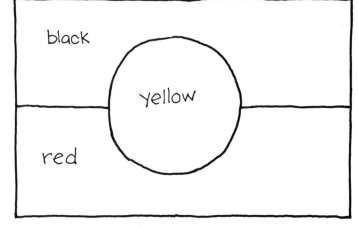

ABORIGINE

Name _____

FURTHER STUDY FOR CHILDREN AROUND THE WORLD

World Children's Day
A 9-year-old girl originated the idea, and she so impressed the United Nations that World Children's Day was begun in 1986. It is celebrated the fourth Sunday in April every year. A theme for the year is announced in September. For more information write: The World Children's Day Foundation, 4401-A Connecticut Avenue, Suite 287, Washington, DC 20008.

By Bread Alone
Every country has a form of bread, be it rice, tortillas, or baguettes. Learn about them and taste them.

Rolling Down the River
Study the major rivers on each continent, how they aid in commerce, and what a trip down that river would be like (Nile, Volga, Ganges, Rhine, Yangtze, Mississippi, Amazon, etc.).

Making Masks
Ancient native cultures the world over use masks for celebrations and religious ceremonies. Learn about various masks and the people who make them. Make masks yourself.

We Are the World
Children dress up like people from various countries. They act the part and tell about the culture of their country. (They might dress up a doll or stuffed animal instead.)

Where Did I Come From?
Encourage children to explore their own roots and share the food and customs of their families.

Capping It Off
Different hats are worn by people in different countries. Learn about them and make copies of them for children to wear.

A Different Tongue
Learn words in different languages and how to write them. Have children learn how to write their names in different alphabets from other cultures.

Happy Days, Holidays
Each country and religion has special holidays. Learn about them and the manner in which they are celebrated. Compare and contrast them with your own culture. Stage some of the celebrations.

A Change of Scenery
Cut pieces of white butcher paper to fit the size of classroom windows. Children draw scenes from different countries on each piece, label them, and put them in the windows. Each window will have a different view.

What A Zoo!
Take a field trip to a zoo and identify the animals and what country and continent they come from.

Mural
Paint a mural of all the countries, customs, and geographies studied.

God Has Many Faces
Visit a synogogue, mosque, cathedral, church, or Buddhist temple. Learn about the practices and beliefs of each of the world's great religions. Find similarities and differences between them.

Bibliography

AUSTRALIA:

Possum Magic by Mem Fox. Nashville, Tennessee: Abingdon Press, 1987.

Wombat Stew by Marcia K. Vaughan. Englewood Cliffs, N.J.: Silver Burdett, 1984.

Aborigines: Down Under* by Jan Reynolds. New York: Harcourt Brace Jovanovich, 1992.

SOUTH AMERICA:

Llama and the Great Flood by Ellen Alexander. New York: Crowell Junior Books, 1989.

This Place Is Wet by Vicki Cobb. New York: Walker and Co., NY, 1989.

Indians of the Amazon** by Marion Morrison. Vero Beach, Florida: Rourke Corp., 1989.

An Adventure in the Amazon by the Cousteau Society. New York: Simon and Schuster, 1992.

EUROPE:

A New Coat for Anna by Harriet Ziefert. New York: Alfred A. Knopf, 1986.

Madeline by Ludwig Bemelmans. New York: Puffin, 1967.

The Story of Ferdinand by Munro Leaf. New York: Puffin, 1964.

Strega Nona by Tomie De Paola. Englewood Cliffs, N.J.: Prentice-Hall, 1975.

The Old Woman Who Lived in a Vinegar Bottle by Rumer Godden. New York: Viking Press, 1970.

Idle Jack by Antony Maitland. New York: Farrar, Straus & Giroux, 1977.

A Family in England*** by Jetty St. John. Minneapolis: Lerner Publications, 1988.

The Twelve Months by Aliki. New York: Greenwillow Books, 1978.

ASIA:

The Dragon Kite of the Autumn Moon by Valerie Reddix. New York: Lothrop, Lee & Shepard Books, 1991.

Nadia the Willful by Sue Alexander. New York: Pantheon Books, 1983.

Min-Yo and the Moon Dragon by Elizabeth Hillman. New York: Harcourt Brace Jovanovich, 1992.

Lon Po Po by Ed Young. New York: Philomel Books, 1989.

The Enchanted Tapestry by Robert D. San Souci. New York: Dial Books, 1987.

The Gift of the Willows by Helena Clare Pittman. Minneapolis: Carolrhoda Books, 1988.

The Papar Crane by Molly Bang. New York: Mulberry Books, 1985.

In the Eyes of the Cat by Demi. New York: Henry Holt & Co., 1992.

Vasilisa the Beautiful by Thomas P. Whitney. New York: Macmillan, 1970.

The Tsar and the Amazing Cow by J. Patrick Lewis. New York: Dial Books, 1988.

Tuan by Eva Boholm-Olsson. New York: R & S Books, 1986.

Ba-Nam by Jeanne M. Lee. New York: Henry Holt & Co., 1987.

Angel Child, Dragon Child by Michele Maria Surat. New York: Scholastic, 1983.

The Girl Who Loved the Wind by Jane Yolen. New York: Harper & Row, 1972.

A Family in India*** by Peter Otto Jacobsen and Kristensen. New York: Bookwright Press, 1984.

The Legend of the Orange Princess by Mehili Gobhai. New York: Holiday House, 1971.

A Gift for the King by Christopher Manson. New York: Henry Holt & Co., 1989.

The Wailing Wall by Leonard Everett Fisher. New York: Macmillan, 1989.

Chicken Man by Michelle Edwards. New York: Lothrop, Lee & Shepard Books, 1991.

Joshua's Dream by Sheila Segal. New York: Union of American Hebrew Congregations, 1985.

NORTH AMERICA:

Riddle of the Drum by Verna Aardema. New York: Four Winds Press, 1979.

Hill of Fire by Thomas P. Lewis. New York: HarperCollins, 1971.

Mary of Mile 18 by Ann Blades. Plattsburg, N.Y.: Tundra Books, 1971.

Pettranella by Betty Waterton. New York: Vanguard Press, 1980.

AFRICA:

The Day of Ahmed's Secret by Florence P. Heide. New York: Lothrop, Lee & Shepard Books, 1990.

The Egyptian Cinderella by Shirley Climo. New York: Crowell Junior Books, 1989.

Bill and Pete by Tomie De Paola. New York: Putnam, 1978.

Bill and Pete Go Down the Nile by Tomie De Paola. New York: Putnam, 1978.

Mummies Made in Egypt by Aliki. New York: Harper & Row, 1979.

Bringing the Rain to Kapiti Plain by Verna Aardema. New York: Dial Books, 1981.

Jambo Means Hello by Muriel Feelings. New York: Dial Books, 1974.

Shadow by Marcia Brown. New York: Charles Scribner's, 1982.

Take a Trip to Nigeria**** by Keith Lye. New York: Franklyn Watts, 1983.

Sahara* by Jan Reynolds. New York: Harcourt Brace Jovanovich, 1991.

Greedy Zebra by Nwenye Hadithi. Boston: Little, Brown & Co., 1984.

Awful Aardvark by Mwalimu & Kennaway. Boston: Little, Brown & Co., 1989.

AROUND THE WORLD:

Festivals Around the World by Philip Steele. Minneapolis: Dillon Press, 1986.

This Is the Way We Go to School by Edith Baer. New York: Scholastic, 1990.

The Way to Start a Day by Byrd Baylor. New York: Charles Scribner's, 1978.

On the Day You Were Born by Debra Frasier. New York: Harcourt Brace Jovanovich, 1991.

Dragons, Dragons by Eric Carle. New York: Philomel Books, 1991.

*   This is part of a series by Jan Reynolds from Harcourt Brace Jovanovich called "Vanishing Cultures." Many other cultures are represented.

**   This is part of a series published by Rourke Publications called "Original Peoples."

***   This is part of a series of books from Bookwright Press called "Families Around the World"; many other countries are represented.

**** This is part of a series published by Franklin Watts, Ltd., called "Take a Trip To." Many other countries are represented.